M000278694

UNLIMITED
ANOINTING

DENNIS GOLDSWORTHY-DAVIS

UNLIMITED
ANOINTING

SECRETS TO OPERATING
—— *in the* ——
FULLNESS OF GOD'S POWER

© Copyright 2018—Dennis Goldsworthy-Davis

All rights reserved. This book is protected by the copyright laws of the United States of America. This book may not be copied or reprinted for commercial gain or profit. The use of short quotations or occasional page copying for personal or group study is permitted and encouraged. Permission will be granted upon request. Unless otherwise identified, Scripture quotations are taken from THE HOLY BIBLE, NEW INTERNATIONAL VERSION®, NIV® Copyright© 1973, 1978, 1984, 2011 by Biblica, Inc.® Used by permission. All rights reserved worldwide. Scripture quotations marked NKJV are from the New King James Version®. Copyright© 1982 by Thomas Nelson. Used by permission. All rights reserved. Scripture quotations marked KJV are from the King James Version. All emphasis within Scripture quotations is the author's own.

DESTINY IMAGE® PUBLISHERS, INC.

P.O. Box 310, Shippensburg, PA 17257-0310

"Promoting Inspired Lives."

This book and all other Destiny Image and Destiny Image Fiction books are available at Christian bookstores and distributors worldwide.

Cover design by Eileen Rockwell
Interior design by Terry Clifton

For more information on foreign distributors, call 717-532-3040.

Or reach us on the Internet: www.destinyimage.com

ISBN 13 TP: 978-0-7684-1931-3
ISBN 13 EBook: 978-0-7684-1932-0
ISBN HC: 978-0-7684-1934-4
ISBN LP: 978-0-7684-1933-7

For Worldwide Distribution, Printed in the U.S.A.
2 3 4 5 6 / 22 21

DEDICATION

To my wife, Christine, without whose support I would never have traveled this journey.

ACKNOWLEDGMENTS

Thank you to...

My original pastor Bennie Finch, for teaching me so much about the anointing.

Paul Keith Davis, for prophesying to me so many years ago concerning writing. It awakened my heart to the possibility.

Jeannie Pircher, for helping so much and in so many ways.

Robert Henderson, for his continual encouragement and help.

CONTENTS

FOREWORD

I have known Dennis Goldsworthy-Davis for the better part of twenty years. In all this time, there is one thing that has characterized his life—his passion for the presence and anointing of God. I know of no one better to write a book about *Unlimited Anointing* than Dennis. I have witnessed his passion for this realm, his function in it, and his desire to impart it to others.

It might be a surprise to some believers to realize there are many anointings. In this book, Dennis discusses some of the anointings that he personally has walked in and carried. Even Jesus, in talking about the coming of the Holy

Spirit in John 7:37-38 (NKJV), speaks of *rivers* of God, not just a river:

> *On the last day, that great day of the feast, Jesus stood and cried out, saying, "If anyone thirsts, let him come to Me and drink. He who believes in Me, as the Scripture has said, out of his heart will flow **rivers** of living water."*

These rivers are the different anointings that the Holy Spirit can bring into our lives. Notice also that it is for the thirsty that these rivers will come to and flow through. Thirsty people are the ones who get anointings from the Lord. This book does just that. It creates a thirst in your spirit for the supernatural of God. It will make you dissatisfied with simply the natural way of living. It will make you long for that which is not of this world.

The anointings of the Holy Spirit are used by God to bring applications into our lives of everything Jesus died for us to have. I have often called the Holy Spirit the "Delivery System" of God. This is not meant to minimize or offend the person of the Holy Spirit. He is to be reverenced and esteemed at all cost. However, in an effort to describe His function, I have chosen this term. He is here to apply and make available to us everything Jesus paid for. This is one of His main purposes on the earth today. He has come to reveal and magnify Jesus and His work. John 16:13-14 (NKJV) reveals Jesus telling us of the Spirit's function:

> *However, when He, the Spirit of truth, has come, He will guide you into all truth; for He will not speak on His own authority, but whatever He hears He will speak; and He will tell you things to come. He will glorify Me, for He will take of what is Mine and declare it to you.*

The Holy Spirit through the anointings of God will take of what Jesus died to provide and declare it to us. This means we get healed, delivered, Fathered, saved, and made whole in every dimension of our lives. This is through the Holy Spirit and His anointings bringing application of all Jesus died for us to have. This is why we must not be ignorant of the Spirit and His ways. This is what the apostle Paul wrote in First Corinthians 12:1 (NKJV), *"Now concerning spiritual gifts, brethren, I do not want you to be ignorant."*

Paul urged us to be aware of the way the Holy Spirit moved and operated so we could get the full benefit of all that is ours. It is the Spirit who brings this into reality. Unless we are aware of the anointings Dennis speaks of in this book, we can potentially miss out on what God has for us.

My exhortation to you: read this book with your spirit wide open and available to God. Let the power of the Spirit come upon you as it did on Jesus (Luke 4:14). Who knows what anointings the Lord has for you to carry. It will change your life and the life of many you will touch.

Blessings,
Robert Henderson

INTRODUCTION

In the incredible encounter of Moses with the Lord on Mount Sinai, the Lord speaks of placing limits around the mountain.

> *Put limits for the people around the mountain and tell them, "Be careful that you do not approach the mountain or touch the foot of it. Whoever touches the mountain is to be put to death"* (Exodus 19:12).

These limits were to stop the people crossing to where the Lord's glory was manifesting. Only Moses was given permission to go all the way into this glory. In other words, the glory was off limits to the general populace. Throughout the Old Testament it stayed that way. But not so today! *The limits are off!* We are told in Hebrews 12, we are not coming to the mountain of the Old Testament—the one with limits...

> *You have not come to a mountain that can be touched and that is burning with fire; to darkness, gloom and storm; to a trumpet blast or to such a voice speaking words that those who heard it begged that no further word be spoken to them, because they could not bear what was commanded: "If even an animal touches the mountain, it must be stoned to death." The sight was so terrifying that Moses said, "I am trembling with fear"* (Hebrews 12:18-21).

...but to the new mountain—Mount Zion. We are coming to the heavenly Jerusalem.

> *But you have come to Mount Zion, to the city of the living God, the heavenly Jerusalem. You have come to thousands upon thousands of angels in joyful assembly"* (Hebrews 12:22).

That which was untouchable is untouchable no more. Jesus brought access and sonship. He released the precious Holy Spirit among us. Paul wrote to the Corinthian church:

> *Now if the ministry that brought death, which was engraved in letters on stone, came with glory, so that the Israelites could not look steadily at the face of Moses because of its glory, transitory though it was, will not the ministry of the Spirit be even more glorious? If the ministry that brought condemnation was glorious, how much more glorious is the ministry that brings righteousness! For what was glorious has no glory now in comparison with the surpassing glory. And if what was transitory came with glory, how much greater is the glory of that which lasts!"* (2 Corinthians 3:7-11)

That which Moses had was glorious, but what comes with the ministry of the Spirit is even more glorious! Paul then speaks of this ministry in depth and starts chapter 4 with this incredible statement: *"Therefore, since through God's mercy we have this ministry, we do not lose heart"* (2 Cor. 4:1). This more glorious ministry, this limitless ministry, is available to all. But will all avail themselves of it?

A great statement is made in Hosea, *"My people are destroyed from lack of knowledge..."* (Hosea 4:6).

Sometimes ignorance and lack of revelation cause us to miss the best of God. This book is part of my personal revelation into the subject of the incredible realm of the anointings of God. Wait! Did I say, "anointings"? Yes, "anointings." More than one! The dictionary won't even let you use the word in plural and yet God's Word itself shows more than one anointing available to the believer.

How did I stumble upon this truth? The Spirit of Truth Himself loves to lead us into all truth and will speak— if we want to listen. Of course, we want to listen! Who wouldn't? Perhaps many, as every letter to the churches in the second chapter of Revelation begins, *"Whoever has ears, let them hear what the Spirit says to the churches..."* (Rev. 2:7,11,17). That statement alone tells us that not all want to hear; nevertheless, the Lord wants to speak to all who will.

So, it is for me. The truth came, of course, through my study of the Word; but specifically, when the Holy Spirit spoke to me one day while on my prayer walk and said, "I want you to minister on the anointings of the believer."

I instantly wanted to argue and wanted to say, "Anointings? You mean anointing!" But I knew the voice of the One speaking. The revelation was on and the journey taking a new direction.

My desire for this book is to share with others as the Holy Spirit reveals more and more truth of what His anointings do. We certainly don't want to live our lives with less than has been prepared for us. I personally love this Scripture in John:

> *He came to that which was his own, but his own did not receive him. Yet to all who did receive him, to those who believed in his name, he gave the right [power and authority] to become children of God* (John 1:11-12).

Love it! The door is open! It makes all that God has available. The table mentioned in Psalm 23:5 can be freshly viewed—all we need is revelation of what is ours and the understanding of how to receive it, and we walk in fresh anointing. It is like when the Lord said to Abraham:

> *Lift your eyes now and look from the place where you are—northward, southward, eastward, and westward; for all the land which you see*

I will give to you and your descendants forever
(Genesis 13:14 NKJV).

Where we are can often be so limiting, but let's look again and let the Holy Spirit show us all that there is to see. He wants to give us what we see! Are we willing to take off our own limits and step into the limitless arena of the ministry of the Holy Spirit? The Word states so beautifully, *"He who began the good work in you, will carry it on to completion"* (Phil. 1:6).

God clearly wants to take us into fullness. This is what I want and I pray that I can encourage others with everything I see. May this book be a source of blessing and encouragement to all whom the Lord wants to read it.

1

UNDERSTANDING THE WORD "ANOINTING"

The first time the word "anointing" jumped out at me was when, as a young believer, I read the Book of Isaiah in the Bible. The prophet Isaiah wrote of the coming Messiah, *"The Spirit of the Sovereign Lord is on me because the Lord has anointed me to..."* (Isa. 61:1). This prophecy was, of course, fulfilled in the life of Jesus and was highlighted in Luke 4 when Jesus quoted Isaiah 61:1-2 and then said, *"Today this scripture is fulfilled in your hearing"* (Luke 4:21).

Luke 4:14 says that, *"Jesus returned from the desert in the power of the Spirit."* A few things can be observed in these statements. First, it was the Spirit of the Sovereign Lord coming upon Jesus who brought the anointing. Second, the anointing was for a reason. He was "anointed to...." Third, He moved in the power of the Spirit. Fourth, He knew He was anointed!

The word used in the Hebrew here for "anointing" or "to anoint" means *to rub on* or *to paint*. This word has a permanency about it. When something is rubbed on or painted on, it becomes one with the object. Although we read in the Old Testament quite often that the Spirit of God moved on people and anointed them for a moment, the actual word, by definition, has a far more permanent connotation.

For centuries, many women have artistically applied makeup by rubbing and massaging oils and lotions into their skin. And men usually use after-shave lotion. Notice the statement, "rubbing and massaging into their skin"? This is said in the sense they are anointing themselves with these oils. So it is with the Holy Spirit! When He anoints, He makes it part of us by infusing us with His oil!

So the anointing becomes part of us and in a sense belongs to us as we walk in those things we are anointed to do.

Truthfully, people in the Old Testament could be anointed for a moment; but most, when anointed in an office, walked with more permanency. Moving into the New Testament, things change. As we continue in Isaiah 61, we read what the anointing on Jesus would do and the power of His ministry; but verse 3 is awesome and very awakening. Those to whom He had ministered and had received Him, He would plant for the display of His splendor. They would manifest His glory!

> *...They will be called oaks of righteousness, a planting of the Lord for the display of his splendor* (Isaiah 61:3).

As the Word delivered to the Colossians says, *"Christ in you, the hope of glory"* (Col. 1:27).

To manifest, it means that the anointing that Jesus had would be available to the ones who received! That's why this great promise of John was so pertinent:

> *And I will ask the Father, and he will give you another advocate to help you and be with you forever—the Spirit of truth. The world cannot*

accept him, because it neither sees him nor knows him. But you know him, for he lives with you and will be in you (John 14:16-17).

The way of the Holy Spirit was now opened, and with Him comes the anointing, or shall we say *anointings*. The Anointer being involved in our lives can only be who He is—the Anointer! He comes, sent directly from Jesus.

Exalted to the right hand of God, he has received from the Father the promised Holy Spirit and has poured out what you now see and hear (Acts 2:33).

He comes with all that He is and all that He can do. But Paul tells us clearly in Ephesians that those things that were at one time mysteries, were now revealed. In fact, in the New International Version of the Bible, the word "mystery" is used seven times in the same book. The Holy Spirit wants to reveal all that there is in this great truth of anointing and anointings!

I feel like Oliver Twist, in Charles Dickens' book, saying, "Please, sir, can I have more?" It had never been heard of before, that one should ask for more. But more is our portion and more is our request! Stirred by the potential, we cry, "MORE!"

2

THE BELIEVER'S ANOINTING

As mentioned previously, in Colossians there is an incredible statement and promise, *"Christ in you, the hope of glory"* (Col. 1:27). Christ, the Anointed One, in you!

First, we are told in Romans that if we have the Spirit of Christ, we belong to Christ.

> *You, however, are not in the realm of the flesh but are in the realm of the Spirit, if indeed **the Spirit of God lives in you**. And if anyone does*

not have the Spirit of Christ, they do not belong
to Christ (Romans 8:9).

It says, *"the Spirit of God lives in you,"* and goes on to say that the manifestation of the Spirit is *"the Spirit of Christ"* himself. The same Anointed One lives in us. So simply, when we receive the Lord, it is not just the Spirit of Jesus alone, it is also His anointing that comes to reside in us.

This releases the second great statement from Colossians, *"Christ in you, the hope of glory"!* The One who transforms us from glory to glory is now at work in us.

> *And we all, who with unveiled faces contemplate*
> *the Lord's glory, are being transformed into his*
> *image with ever-increasing glory, which comes*
> *from the Lord, who is the Spirit* (2 Corinthians
> 3:18).

One translation of the word "glory" is the "weighty presence of God." That means the manifested presence of God!

This anointing, which I have called "the believer's anointing," is available to all believers! It is for all who receive Him. All the potential of God is simply released through this wonderful anointing. In the language of the

NIV translation of the Bible, it is called an *anointing* (or *an unction*) from the Holy One.

> *But you have an **anointing** from the Holy One,*
> *and all of you know the truth* (1 John 2:20).

The anointing from the Holy One causes us to know the truth. And we are told in verse 27, speaking of the same anointing, that the anointing teaches us.

> *As for you, the anointing you received from him remains in you, and you do not need anyone to teach you. But as **his anointing teaches you** about all things and as that anointing is real, not counterfeit—just as it has taught you, remain in him* (1 John 2:27).

The Spirit of Truth anoints us as believers to know truth, and continues to teach us truth. To add a personal note here: When I was called by the Lord into the ministry, this very Scripture was given to me prophetically while praying about whether or not I should attend Bible school. I never went, but He was faithful to His word to me and taught me, revealing truth after truth and enabling me to minister that same truth. He has been faithful for more than forty years to this promise! The last statement regarding enabling, we will cover in an upcoming chapter.

In the Old Testament, an offering or sacrifice had to be mixed with oil to be acceptable to God. The following are two examples of Scriptures concerning this:

> *And from the finest wheat flour make round loaves without yeast, thick loaves without yeast and with olive oil mixed in, and thin loaves without yeast and brushed with olive oil* (Exodus 29:2).

> *With the first lamb offer a tenth of an ephah of the finest flour mixed with a quarter of a hin of oil from pressed olives, and a quarter of a hin of wine as a drink offering* (Exodus 29:40).

This offering, or sacrifice, was so prophetic of what would happen in the New Testament. When all believers anointed with the Spirit of Christ would come to worship, their worship would be accepted because the One who opened the way has released His anointing into us. The Father accepts because we are anointed by His Spirit to stand before Him. When we receive Him, His blood cleanses our sin and His anointing, the *"Christ in you,"* releases acceptance before our God.

Truthfully, the hope of glory? We get to stand in the presence of the One who is the glory and ministers from the glory. David said it so beautifully, *"You will fill me with joy in your presence, with eternal pleasures at your right hand"* (Ps. 16:11).

The scope and magnitude of this awesome truth, the potential released, and the possibilities are nothing less than a lifetime of experience opened to us and revealed to us by such an anointing! That's why we are told that when we receive Him, He gives us the authority to become the children of God: *"Yet to all who did receive him, to those who believed in his name, he gave the right to become children of God"* (John 1:12).

His anointing in us releases sonship and reveals sonship and all that the inheritance of that truth means: *"he predestined us for adoption to sonship through Jesus Christ, in accordance with his pleasure and will"* (Eph. 1:5).

There is another tremendous blessing that this anointing releases in the New Testament believer. Back in the Old Testament era, a priest could not minister to the Lord without being anointed and ordained to do so.

> *After you put these clothes on your brother Aaron and his sons, anoint and ordain them. Consecrate them so they may serve me as priests* (Exodus 28:41).

This was a lasting ordinance cited in Exodus 28. Aaron and his sons had to be consecrated to minister. But in the New Testament, this honor is given to all believers. The consecration and anointing of the Christ within us releases us to become priests of the Lord, where we minister to Him and for Him, as indeed the Old Testament priests did. This is clearly spelled out in the New Testament, specifically in First Peter:

> *You also, like living stones, are being built into a spiritual house to be a holy priesthood, offering spiritual sacrifices acceptable to God through Jesus Christ* (1 Peter 2:5).

> *But you are a chosen people, a royal priesthood, a holy nation, God's special possession, that you may declare the praises of him who called you out of darkness into his wonderful light* (1 Peter 2:9).

We are told we are a holy priesthood that is to offer spiritual sacrifices in verse 5 and a royal priesthood that declares His praises or virtues in verse 9. To Him and for Him!

Revelation declares that we are kings and priests unto God: "...To him who loves us and has freed us from our sins by his blood, and has made us to be a kingdom and priests to serve his God and Father..." (Rev. 1:5-6).

We are to be touched by royalty and touched by anointing. We are His priests for His Kingdom. There is not much greater than that! This is confirmed in Revelation 5:10: *"You have made them to be a kingdom and priests to serve our God, and they will reign on the earth."*

In the Old Testament, just the selected few were selected to be priests. In the New Testament, the chosen people of God for God are anointed as royal priests in His Kingdom.

> *...This inheritance is kept in heaven for you, who through faith are shielded by God's power until the coming of the salvation that is ready to be revealed in the last time* (1 Peter 1:4-5).

What an awesome privilege—what an awesome door to stand before our King and on His behalf!

When we have the Holy Spirit at work in our lives as believers, it opens the door to all that He has and is. He transforms us from glory to glory; but even more, we are told we can manifest that glory.

And we all, who with unveiled faces contemplate the Lord's glory, are being transformed into his image with ever-increasing glory, which comes from the Lord, who is the Spirit (2 Corinthians 3:18).

This same third chapter in Second Corinthians tells us of the ministry of the Spirit that Paul walked in. And in chapter 4, he makes a great statement: *"Therefore, since through God's mercy we have this ministry, we do not lose heart"* (2 Cor. 4:1).

Notice the word, "we"! Not just I, Paul, but *we,* meaning others walk in this same ministry. The believer has the right to walk and manifest the ministry of the Holy Spirit. The next few chapters tell us of some of those anointings that will manifest such a glorious ministry. The Christian life is indeed limitless as we come to know the fullness of the anointings of God. Did not our Savior walk in the sevenfold Spirit of God, as recorded in Isaiah.

The Spirit of the Lord will rest on him—the Spirit of wisdom and of understanding, the Spirit of counsel and of might, the Spirit of the knowledge and fear of the Lord (Isaiah 11:2).

- The Spirit of the Lord

- The Spirit of Wisdom

- The Spirit of Understanding

- The Spirit of Counsel

- The Spirit of Power

- The Spirit of Knowledge

- The fear of the Lord

As previously stated, in Romans 8:9, we are clearly told that we have the Spirit of Christ. We are also told that we are coheirs with Him.

> *Now if we are children, then we are heirs—heirs of God and co-heirs with Christ, if indeed we share in his sufferings in order that we may also share in his glory* (Romans 8:17).

Meaning that all He has gained is ours as children of God to gain and walk. All that by the same One who anointed Him.

> *The Spirit of the Sovereign Lord is on me, because the Lord has anointed me to proclaim good news to the poor. He has sent me to bind up the brokenhearted, to proclaim freedom for the*

captives and release from darkness for the prisoners (Isaiah 61:1).

This is the One who anoints the believer.

3

THE ANOINTINGS
OF JESUS

*T*he Spirit of the living God is upon me and he anointed me to..." is such a great motivation for us today. Jesus, the Son of God, relied on the anointing to minister. Why? Because even though in nature God, He became a man so that as a man He would conquer sin, and as a man would fulfill His ministry. He was showing us, as men and women, what we could walk in as we begin to minister. Several verses later in Isaiah 61 is a particular promise that shares that:

> *...to bestow on them a crown of beauty instead of ashes, the oil of joy instead of mourning, and*

*a garment of praise instead of a spirit of despair.
They will be called oaks of righteousness, a
planting of the Lord for the display of his splendor* (Isaiah 61:3).

Those who have received His ministry can in turn display His ministry and splendor!

But to look at what Jesus was anointed to do shares such
a scope of the anointing's ability in one man. He told the
disciples that He wanted us to walk in the same works and
even greater works. How? By the same anointing!

*Very truly I tell you, whoever believes in me will
do the works I have been doing, and they will
do even greater things than these, because I am
going to the Father* (John 14:12).

So looking at Jesus' anointings opens the door to the
full realm of all that this means. The sevenfold Spirit of
God spoken of in Isaiah 11 and mentioned in the previous
chapter was His portion.

*The Spirit of the Lord will rest on him—the
Spirit of wisdom and of understanding, the
Spirit of counsel and of might, the Spirit of the
knowledge and fear of the Lord* (Isaiah 11:2).

This so clearly manifested throughout Jesus' ministry.

The Spirit of the sovereign Lord, the Spirit of wisdom and understanding, the Spirit of counsel, and of power. The Spirit of knowledge and of the fear of the Lord. All of these manifested continually throughout Jesus' ministry. But for this portion of the book, we will concentrate on what was promised in Isaiah 61:1-3 and, of course, proclaimed in Luke 4:18-20, previously referenced.

First, anointed to preach. To preach God's indelible word needs an anointing from Him to do such a noble task. Many can speak or give presentations, but this is different. In its root explanation of the word "preach," the dictionary says *to publicly deliver a sermon,* not just give a talk. Jesus, as so many after Him, relied on the anointing to release the word of a God to the hearers. He opened the door to the ministry of preaching the Gospel and good news to those who would hear.

Second, the ministry to "proclaim" means to *announce and pronounce, to declare officially, as to bring into being.* Jesus was anointed to bring about the proclamations of all that God had said and was releasing in that hour and ever since. This has a prophetic element in it and a knowing of the present word of God. This proclamation also had such an authority that it would set captives free. An anointing that would, by simple proclamation, bring deliverance and freedom. As written in Acts:

> *You know what has happened throughout the province of Judea, beginning in Galilee after the baptism that John preached—how **God anointed Jesus** of Nazareth with the Holy Spirit and power, and how he went around doing good and healing all who were under the power of the devil, because God was with him* (Acts 10:37-38).

It also speaks of the realm of bringing light into darkness, which Jesus was to the world: "In him was life, and that life was the light of all mankind. The light shines in the darkness, and the darkness has not overcome it" (John 1:4-5).

Back to Isaiah 61:1, it says Jesus was sent to *"bind up the brokenhearted."* "Bind up" means *to wrap firmly or heal and to saddle up,* as to so heal that they can carry His healing and life to others.

So far, we have anointings to preach, deliver, and heal the inward person, so as to be ready to do the same. But there is yet more! We are then told to comfort those who mourn. The Holy Spirit, the Comforter, anoints to comfort! This word "comfort" has within its meaning *compassion* and *to bring ease* and even *to avenge the pain*. That is why in the description of *prophecy* in First Corinthians, we are told one of the attributes is *comfort*.

> *But the one who prophesies speaks to people for their strengthening, encouraging and comfort* (1 Corinthians 14:3).

Alongside this anointing, we are told to provide for those who grieve and to bestow a crown of beauty for ashes and the oil of joy for mourning and a garment of praise for the spirit of despair. The anointing to comfort has the ability to replace the pain with none other than the anointing of salvation and royalty.

Of course, this is just a short description of the anointings of Jesus as described in Isaiah 61. It was public and yet personal. He delivered and healed and reequipped. He then released others to do the same! So, we cannot avoid the great promise of Jesus in the Book of John:

> *On the last and greatest day of the festival, Jesus stood and said in a loud voice, "Let anyone who is thirsty come to me and drink. Whoever believes in me, as Scripture has said, rivers of*

living water will flow from within them" (John 7:37-38).

This anointing cannot be contained, it flows like rivers and affects all it touches and causes them to come under the same Anointer! What Jesus did from His overflow, others who are anointed can also do. Look at Paul with the Ephesian church as told in Acts:

> *While Apollos was at Corinth, Paul took the road through the interior and arrived at Ephesus. There he found some disciples and asked them, "Did you receive the Holy Spirit when you believed?" They answered, "No, we have not even heard that there is a Holy Spirit." So Paul asked, "Then what baptism did you receive?" "John's baptism," they replied. Paul said, "John's baptism was a baptism of repentance. He told the people to believe in the one coming after him, that is, in Jesus." On hearing this, they were baptized in the name of the Lord Jesus* (Acts 19:1-5).

This Scripture passage, of course, cannot completely describe the fullness of the realms of our Lord's great anointings. He was anointed as the Chief Apostle and the Great High Priest. He carried all the fivefold ministries, as mentioned in Ephesians. It would probably take more than one book to describe and cover such realms, but the purpose is to show what is available to the believer. There are no limits to what the Lord had and has released for us to have when we consider His promises to us; and again, note that Jesus is promising this in John:

> *Very truly I tell you, whoever believes in me will do the works I have been doing, and they will do even greater things than these, because I am going to the Father* (John 14:12).

He promised that we would do greater works!

4

ANOINTED BY THE ANOINTER

Jesus clearly proves in Luke that the famous Scripture of Isaiah 61 is speaking of Him:

> *The Spirit of the Lord is on me, because he has anointed me to proclaim good news to the poor. He has sent me to proclaim freedom for the prisoners and recovery of sight for the blind, to set the oppressed free, to proclaim the year of the Lord's favor* [Luke's quote from Isaiah 61:1-3]. *Then he* [Jesus] *rolled up the scroll, gave it back to the attendant and sat down. The eyes of everyone in the synagogue were fastened on him. He*

began by saying to them, "Today this scripture is fulfilled in your hearing" (Luke 4:18-21).

The Spirit of the Sovereign Lord is upon Me and He has anointed Me, proclaimed Jesus! Jesus didn't need the Spirit of Christ. He was and is the Christ! He was and is the Savior anointed. And this is the anointing that He would subsequently release on the Church.

Exalted to the right hand of God, he has received from the Father the promised Holy Spirit and has poured out what you now see and hear (Acts 2:33).

> *The promise of the Father! The Spirit who anointed Him would be released to anoint the church.*

This anointing has many names and many descriptions. One description, the Baptism of the Spirit, is spoken of by Jesus: *"For John baptized with water, but in a few days you will be baptized with the Holy Spirit"* (Acts 1:5).

This explains the depth of the anointing that would be released. The word "baptism" in its original language is the Greek word *baptizō*. It means *to make fully wet or immersed*, hence the anointing. Another meaning is *to be overwhelmed*. It is the same word used to dye a garment.

Remember the word "anoint" and its meaning *to rub in or to paint?* It comes through baptism. To be immersed in, overwhelmed, and thoroughly soaked and wet.

I remember having a discussion with my pastor when I was born again. He had told me that I needed to be baptized. I told him I had already been baptized. "When?" he asked. "When I was a baby, I was baptized in the church of Ireland," I said. "Oh no!" he proclaimed. "That act was a christening. Baptism is being fully immersed in water. That was only a sprinkling!" Oh! I wonder how many Christians miss out on the immersion of the Anointer Himself because they think a touch, a sprinkling of God is enough?

Another tremendous description on this anointing is given in Acts 10:

> *You know what has happened throughout the province of Judea, beginning in Galilee after the baptism that John preached—how God anointed Jesus of Nazareth with the Holy Spirit and power, and how he went around doing good and healing all who were under the power of the devil, because God was with him* (Acts 10:37-38).

The anointing of the Holy Spirit brings power! The Greek word for "power" is *dunamis*. This is the word from which we get our English word "dynamite." Its function, mentioned in the same verse, is to heal all who were oppressed by the devil. The anointing of power had function. It healed all that the devil had done. But this anointing was not just for Jesus. He gave this promise:

> *"For John baptized with water, but in a few days you will be baptized with the Holy Spirit." Then they gathered around him and asked him, "Lord, are you at this time going to restore the kingdom to Israel?" He said to them: "It is not for you to know the times or dates the Father has set by his own authority. But you will receive power when the Holy Spirit comes on you; and you will be my witnesses in Jerusalem, and in all Judea and Samaria, and to the ends of the earth"* (Acts 1:5-8).

Jesus told the disciples that when they were baptized in the Holy Spirit, they would receive the same *dunamis*. The same power! As a result, they would be witnesses of Jesus the Christ. They would witness by manifesting His power in Jerusalem and Judaea and Samaria and the whole world.

They did that so incredibly that, in fact, one verse says, quoting King James Version:

> *And when they found them not, they drew Jason and certain brethren unto the rulers of the city, crying, These that have turned the world upside down are come hither also* (Acts 17:6).

The same power. The same results. This is the power of the baptism of the Spirit. Another promise concerning this baptism is found in Luke:

> *I am going to send you what my Father has promised; but stay in the city until you have been clothed with power from on high* (Luke 24:49).

Clothed with power from on high! The word "clothed" used by the NIV here is a great description. Clothed, meaning *anointed, rubbed on, and painted.* Awesome! But notice the words *"power from on high."* This phrase is clearly defining that the baptism of the Spirit is a power encounter and a power anointing! We must not limit this incredible anointing to a weakened version when it is a Jesus-promised version! Not limited to the day of Pentecost alone!

> *The promise is for you and your children and for all who are far off—for all whom the Lord our God will call* (Acts 2:39).

This promise includes the modern-day church. I once saw an amazing sight. A major power line, carrying power across Texas, was hit by lightning. The result? A blue flame leaped in the air with a major sound and smoke. The power from on high was greater than the power below. This is our promise! The promise of a greater power than the greatest power we could muster or deem to carry.

This same baptism, or anointing, carries with it the abilities of God. The word *dunamis* itself carries not just *power* but also *ability*. When this anointing comes, the Anointer comes. His abilities and gifts come with Him. Hence the statement in Isaiah 61:1, *"And he has anointed me to...."*

5

ANOINTED TO AND INTO AN OFFICE

There are some stories in the Old Testament that, for me, have such a dynamic affect. I suspect that is due to the realm God has given me to walk in. One such story is found in First Samuel 16:1-13. The Lord tells Samuel to fill his horn with oil and go to Jesse to anoint one of his sons.

> *The Lord said to Samuel, "How long will you mourn for Saul, since I have rejected him as king over Israel? Fill your horn with oil and be on your way; I am sending you to Jesse of*

> *Bethlehem. I have chosen one of his sons to be*
> *king"* (1 Samuel 16:1).

This is the second time the Lord has told Samuel to anoint a coming king. The first time is David's predecessor, Saul. Unlike with Saul, whom God had sent to Samuel, this time it was Samuel's job to go to him. For Samuel, this was a prophet's nightmare. Why? There's nothing like being told to anoint someone, but you don't know who it is you are about to anoint. This chapter in Samuel is filled with gems, but here is the truth of this anointing. In both cases of Saul and David, they were called and ordained by God to function in the office of king, but God would not release them until they had been anointed into that office. Priests in the Old Testament could not function until they were anointed.

> *After you put these clothes on your brother*
> *Aaron and his sons, **anoint** and ordain them.*
> *Consecrate them so they may serve me as priests*
> (Exodus 28:41).

"Anoint and ordain them." Kings could not function without being anointed. It is evident in both this passage and First Kings.

*The Lord said to him, "Go back the way you came, and go to the Desert of Damascus. When you get there, **anoint** Hazael king over Aram. Also, anoint Jehu son of Nimshi king over Israel, and **anoint** Elisha son of Shaphat from Abel Meholah to succeed you as prophet* (1 Kings 19:15-16).

Elijah is told to anoint two kings. He was told also to operate in the office of a prophet. In these same verses, Elijah is told to anoint a prophet to replace him, Elisha. So no matter what the call, the anointing was needed to function. Jesus Himself did not fully operate until He was anointed to do so.

There is a very interesting truth also found in the anointing of David that we should observe.

*So Samuel took the horn of oil and **anointed him** [David] in the presence of his brothers, and from that day on **the Spirit of the Lord came powerfully upon David**. Samuel then went to Ramah* (1 Samuel 16:13).

First truth, the anointing empowers to operate. Without it, we are just wannabes.

Second truth, David was anointed in front of his brothers. When anointed into an office, the anointing should be done in the presence of your brothers and those familiar with you, who knew you before and after the anointing took place. Also the anointing should take place in the presence of believers in Christ so that you are recognized as one chosen by God.

In today's church, so many are claiming that they are "this office" and "that office" but if their anointing does not stand out among the others, it is no more than a mere claim! A title that is self-proclaimed is one thing, but an anointing to operate in that office is another.

King Uzziah, in Second Chronicles 26:16-21, is a good example and more so a clear warning, concerning this. He stepped outside his office of king and began to offer the sacrifices only the anointed priests could offer. The passage tells us that when the priests confronted him, he became angry; and as he did, leprosy broke out on his forehead—thus condemning him to a life of seclusion. And his son had to take his place.

King Saul, famous for being David's predecessor, did the same thing and the prophet Samuel had to rebuke him in First Samuel 15:17-28. In fact, during his rebuke,

Samuel told King Saul, *"Although you were once small in your own eyes...."* Often enough when anointed there is such a danger of pride! The saddest statement though is found in verse 28:

> *Samuel said to him, "The Lord has torn the kingdom of Israel from you today and has given it to one of your neighbors—to one better than you"* (1 Samuel 15:28).

The whole Book of First Samuel is quite worth a read!

In the New Testament church, other offices came into being that needed equal anointing. As the Holy Spirit came on Jesus to anoint Him into both office and function, so He has released the Holy Spirit upon the Church to anoint in the same manner. The offices of the fivefold ministry are recorded in Ephesians.

> *So Christ himself gave the **apostles**, the **prophets**, the **evangelists**, the **pastors** and **teachers**, to equip his people for works of service, so that the body of Christ may be built up until we all reach unity in the faith and in the knowledge of the Son of God and become mature, attaining to the whole measure of the fullness of Christ* (Ephesians 4:11-13).

Two things are important to note here: who gave them and how many were given. If Christ didn't ordain it, will He anoint it? Equally, the word "some" is used, which implies a definite *not all*. Not all are to hold these offices, but some are! If so, they will be ordained and anointed by the Holy Spirit to operate in such an office.

The offices of the New Testament are not limited to these mentioned here. Both Romans 12 and First Corinthians 12 speak of other offices—all called and all needing the anointing to function, such as leadership, administrations, and worship.

Joshua was anointed to be the leader in Moses' stead.

> *Now Joshua son of Nun was filled with the spirit of wisdom because Moses had laid his hands on him. So the Israelites listened to him and did what the Lord had commanded Moses* (Deuteronomy 34:9).

David was anointed in the realm of worship in incredible ways. Can one be anointed in more than one office? Clearly so! Paul was anointed as a leader, an apostle, a herald, and a teacher. He mentions it twice to Timothy.

> *And for this purpose I was appointed a herald and an apostle—I am telling the truth, I am*

not lying—and a true and faithful teacher of the Gentiles (1 Timothy 2:7).

And of this gospel I was appointed a herald and an apostle and a teacher (2 Timothy 1:11).

The anointing of both David and Elisha have a significant revelation that is necessary to point out. Both of them were actually anointed several times. First, they were anointed *to* the office and then they were anointed *in* the office. David was anointed to be king in First Samuel 16, but then twice more when ordained into full kingship. He was ordained both for Judah and then all of Israel.

*Then the men of Judah came to Hebron, and there they **anointed** David king over the tribe of Judah* (2 Samuel 2:4).

*When all the elders of Israel had come to King David at Hebron, the king made a covenant with them at Hebron before the Lord, and they **anointed** David king over Israel* (2 Samuel 5:3).

Elisha was anointed to be a prophet when the cloak of the prophet was thrown on him, and again when he picked up that same cloak to own and possess for himself.

So Elijah went from there and found Elisha son of Shaphat. He was plowing with twelve yoke of oxen, and he himself was driving the twelfth pair. Elijah went up to him and threw his cloak around him (1 Kings 19:19).

Elisha then picked up Elijah's cloak that had fallen from him and went back and stood on the bank of the Jordan (2 Kings 2:13).

This is tremendously important for our understanding. God will anoint people into a call and into preparation for their ministry, but they are actually separated to that office, but are not yet to operate in that office. This anointing is imperative and the walk of training is imperative.

In this day of drive-thru food and banking, we want drive-thru anointing. Both David and Elisha waited their due season. How many want the fullness of their call without the due process of that call. They want the fullness of the anointing without the due process that causes us to be ready for that same anointing!

The Lord counts His anointing as imperative and protects it as precious to Himself. He actually calls the anointing oil *"sacred"*:

> *Say to the Israelites, "This is to be my* **sacred** **anointing** *oil for the generations to come"* (Exodus 30:31).

In fact, He says, *"Do not touch my anointed ones; do my prophets no harm"* (1 Chron. 16:22).

David, although Saul persecuted him and hounded him, made this statement about Saul, *"But the Lord forbid that I should lay a hand on the Lord's anointed"* (1 Sam. 26:11).

Why? Because David understood the sacredness of anointing. Today, ministers run down other ministers and people do so to their leaders, not understanding they are touching the sacred! When David found out that a young Amalekite had killed Saul, he was horrified. Read his words:

> *David asked him, "Why weren't you afraid to lift your hand to destroy the Lord's anointed?" Then David called one of his men and said, "Go, strike him down!" So he struck him down, and he died* (2 Samuel 1:14-15).

I wonder how many have ruined their own lives and ministries by not counting sacred the anointing of God while seeking for more of it for themselves? We live in a generation of freedom of speech and lack of honor yet wonder why the anointing is so lacking today.

6

THE BELIEVER'S POTENTIAL

As we have looked at the great statement in Isaiah 61, *"And he has anointed me to,"* it reveals a truth that being "anointed to" is the purpose of the anointing. However, as shown in that passage, the anointing, of course, has particular manifestations. John, writing concerning the anointing, explains the anointing to the readers by making an eye-opening statement, revealing the true purpose of anointing:

> *As for you, the anointing you received from him remains in you, and you do not need anyone to*

> *teach you. But as his anointing teaches you about all things and as that anointing is real, not counterfeit—just as it has taught you, remain in him* (1 John 2:27).

The anointing you have received is real and not a counterfeit. When we receive an anointing to minister, it is for real and it manifests itself—it is not a copy! We can't copy an anointing. If we try to, it is not anointed, it's just actually a shadow of the real thing—as Paul so aptly says, *"These are a shadow of the things that were to come; the reality, however, is found in Christ"* (Col. 2:17).

Some things are shadows and some things are realities. The anointing is the *real thing*—a copy has no substance. Using the old Pentecostal word that we will discuss more fully later, the anointing has an *unction* to it, an *ability* to it, a manifestation to it.

There is a wonderful, true story of a public event where an actor and a preacher both are asked to quote the 23rd Psalm, The Lord is my Shepherd. The actor, using all his abilities, wows the people with his drama and diction. When the preacher quotes it, there is not a dry eye in the place. The difference? The preacher had a knowledge of the Shepherd and the anointing to minister. The actor?

A dramatization of it. Oh for the anointing in what we do! Or better said, oh for the anointing to do what we do. Without the anointing, there is really only an effort to do, but the doing is not really done!

As in the case of Jesus, the "anointings to do" are varied and many. My heart is that we become aware of their potential. There are the anointings of office (as previously mentioned), the anointing to preach, to lead, to administer, etc. Anointing and grace run so beautifully hand in hand. First Corinthians 12 shows some of this variance. Verses 1-11 speak of the spiritual gifts. In fact, there are nine altogether. But verse 7 is the key verse: *"Now to each one the manifestation of the Spirit is given for the common good"* (1 Cor. 12:7).

All nine spiritual gifts are manifestations of the Spirit. Whether permanent or momentary, the anointing of the Spirit is involved! Verses 27-30 in First Corinthians 12, show some of the manifested appointments of God from apostles through to ministering in tongues.

> *Now you are the body of Christ, and each one of you is a part of it. And God has placed in the church first of all **apostles**, second **prophets**, third **teachers**, then **miracles**, then gifts of*

__healing__, of __helping__, of __guidance__, and of different ent kinds of __tongues__. Are all apostles? Are all prophets? Are all teachers? Do all work miracles? Do all have gifts of healing? Do all speak in tongues? Do all __interpret__? Now eagerly desire the greater gifts (1 Corinthians 12:27-30).

These are all appointments that need anointing. You will never be appointed without being anointed.

I do believe, however, that the Lord gives us the key to our areas of anointing in verse 31: *"Now eagerly desire the greater gifts"* (1 Cor. 12:31).

This word "desire" has within it a revelation. It has to do with *a passionate, lusting after.* I believe this is not a natural desire but a spiritual desire! The Holy Spirit within you stirs you to long for that in which He wants to use you and manifest through you. The King James Version says, *"This is a true saying, if a man desire the office of a bishop, he desireth a good work"* (1 Tim. 3:1).

A God-given and God-driven desire! What do you feel passionately stirred about? Pray for the anointing for such a longing!

Two statements in this passage of First Corinthians 12 are quite key to knowing and walking in your "anointing to." One: *"There are different kinds of working, but in all of them and in everyone it is the same God at work"* (1 Cor. 12:6). God works them. The anointing is God working and yet using you as a vessel. This is a great way to know if you are anointed! God works! Have you ever watched someone like Reverend Billy Graham preach? He didn't say anything different from anyone else, but God worked his anointing. Incredible to behold. Many folks can pray for the sick, and then suddenly a person anointed to pray for the sick turns up. Watch the difference in how God works!

Two: The next statement that is quite key, as was previously mentioned, is in verse 7 of First Corinthians 12: *"the manifestation of the Spirit...."* Where there is an anointing, the Holy Spirit will manifest that anointing! It takes the stress out. We are just the earthen vessels, or jars of clay, as Paul states in Second Corinthians 4:7. It is the Holy Spirit's manifestation that counts. I personally love this! He uses us, marred and often somewhat cracked vessels, to display His splendor and glory.

I think it is good to mention again that there can be both momentary and permanent anointings. We know the word "anointing" in essence means *to rub on*. Concerning the word "manifestation," found in First Corinthians

12:7, the actual Greek word used is *phanerōsis* meaning *an expression or exhibition of what is bestowed.* Another rendering is the dancing hand of God. Put the two together and it could read this way: The Holy Spirit dances and exhibits His anointings in those anointed or He could touch with a momentary unction to flow in that particular arena.

How will you know the difference? The resident anointing can be used at any time as we operate our gift by faith. A momentary anointing will have an unction of faith to operate in something that we don't normally flow in.

Also, we need to catch the revelation in this passage of the uniqueness of the anointing. Previous verses speak of the variances of how the Holy Spirit will operate.

> *There are different kinds of gifts, but the same Spirit distributes them. There are different kinds of service, but the same Lord. There are different kinds of working, but in all of them and in everyone it is the same God at work* (1 Corinthians 12:4-6).

Look at the Old Testament prophets. Watch how differently their anointings operated. It is the same today. The Anointer is always the same, but His operations are unique and often crafted around the vessel He uses. The result will always be the hand of God, but what beautiful expressions there will be. Perhaps one of the most unique manifestations of this is told in the story of Bezalel and Oholiab in the Old Testament. They had the Spirit of God within them to enable them to do extraordinary works of craftsmanship.

> *See, I have chosen Bezalel son of Uri, the son of Hur, of the tribe of Judah, and **I have filled him with the Spirit of God**, with wisdom, with understanding, with knowledge and with all kinds of skills—to make artistic designs for work in gold, silver and bronze, to cut and set stones, to work in wood, and to engage in all kinds of crafts. Moreover, **I have appointed** Oholiab son of Ahisamak, of the tribe of Dan, to help him. Also I have given ability to all the skilled workers to make everything I have commanded you* (Exodus 31:2-6).

This passage goes to prove that anointing can also work so powerfully through and in the marketplace.

One of the dangers of those who are *anointed to* minister is that they sometimes rely on that anointing and don't seek to be *anointed in* the very thing that they are anointed to do. For instance, I can be anointed to preach. Indeed, that is an anointing I have. I remember the day and the hour it came. This means I can preach at the drop of a hat, but if I don't ask for the anointing afresh when I preach, it can mean that my anointing will enable me to manifest its gift but I don't flow in the present available anointing while manifesting that gift.

The same can be true of many and varied giftings. We need to not only be *anointed to* but also *anointed in!* Makes you want to sing that wonderful old song, "Oh for a new anointing." Never rely on the old anointing—always rely on the Anointer Himself.

7

THE SHADOW OF OTHERS' ANOINTINGS

I will never forget the story told to us by Bill Johnson, pastor of Bethel Church, as he was ministering alongside a famous prophet, Dick Mills, when he was a younger man. Suddenly Pastor Johnson was called out to prophesy by Dick and stand alongside him. He reports that he was quite scared and said to himself, *I don't prophesy, you do.* And then to his ultimate shock, when he stood next to the prophet, he suddenly found himself operating under the same anointing. He was standing in the prophet's shadow. The anointing has a shadow? It sure does. Remember Peter?

As a result, people brought the sick into the streets and laid them on beds and mats so that at least Peter's shadow might fall on some of them as he passed by (Acts 5:15).

People brought the sick outside and laid them in the street so that they would be touched by Peter's shadow as he passed by. How great was the shadow? It stretched at least across a street. How many feet do you suppose that would be?

I first experienced this spiritual phenomenon as a young man. I had been privileged to become acquainted with a man anointed with the presence of God and was used in healing and deliverance. Meeting him, I could feel the anointing emanate. I invited him into our local church to minister. I stood next to him as he ministered. Not only was I affected by his anointing but its shadow stayed with me for many days after he left. I came under the influence of his anointing. I could minister as he did for that period of time. "Is that biblical?" one might ask? It sure is. Consider these statements from the Old Testament:

When all those who had formerly known him saw him prophesying with the prophets, they asked each other, "What is this that has happened to the son of Kish? Is Saul also among the prophets?" A man who lived there answered, "And who is their father?" So it became a saying: "Is Saul also among the prophets?" (1 Samuel 10:11-12).

He stripped off his garments, and he too prophesied in Samuel's presence. He lay naked all that day and all that night. This is why people say, "Is Saul also among the prophets?" (1 Samuel 19:24).

Is Saul among the prophets? What had happened? Saul the king, who was actually anointed to be king, had come into the presence of a company of prophets. The first time he met them was on his journey home, and the Spirit on them came on him mightily. This momentary anointing lasted while Saul was with them.

The second time, Saul prophesied day and night. Actually, this second time when Saul came under this shadow is a tremendous story. It is found in First Samuel 19:19-24. Saul was determined to capture David, but he was with a company of prophets, including Samuel. In disregard for the very man who had anointed him in the first place, Saul sent men three times to arrest David, but each time as they came near, the anointing was so great on the prophets that as they entered the vicinity where they were, the anointing would hit these men and they began to prophesy.

Saul finally went himself and the same happened to him, even from a distance. Powerful anointing, indeed! What a long shadow it had. In fact, it hit Saul as he came into the vicinity and caused him to lay down for a day and night. He was not a prophet, but came under its shadow.

This truthfully can happen to an individual, or as seen in Saul's men, more than one person at a time. In fact, Jesus sent out the disciples under His anointing. The Spirit had not come on them yet, so they were functioning under Him. Their time came on the day of Pentecost to function under their own anointing, when they received the Spirit for themselves. Perhaps only history will record how many people can come under this shadow at one time and function under it; but I have already seen whole churches affected by the anointing when one carries it so powerfully.

This particular shadow anointing adds a dimension to how limitless the Holy Spirit and the realm of anointing is. There can be a danger if we don't realize from where the anointing operates. We begin to think that we have gained this anointing for ourselves, only to find later that it was in fact the shadow of another's anointing that had fallen upon us. As a young man, I had to learn this lesson more than once, although it sure made me hungry for more. There is nothing quite like being touched by something special, to make you want it for yourself!

8

ANOINTED WITH THE OIL OF JOY

I suppose that anybody who has ever read the Book of Hebrews could not miss this statement:

> *You have loved righteousness and hated wickedness; therefore God, your God, has set you above your companions by **anointing you** with the oil of joy* (Hebrews 1:9).

Therefore, God anointed you with the oil of joy above your companions. This is once again speaking of another of the anointings of Jesus. This anointing imparts the actual joy of the Lord. Clearly there were times in the history of Israel when this was released. Nehemiah makes this statement, *"Go and enjoy choice food and sweet drinks, and send some to those who have nothing prepared. This day is holy to our Lord. Do not grieve, for the joy of the Lord is your strength"* (Neh. 8:10).

Feast days in Israel seem to be accompanied with an impartation of joy! And Nehemiah knew it and wanted the people to enjoy it while it was there. One such feast day manifests when David becomes king.

> *Also, their neighbors from as far away as Issachar, Zebulun and Naphtali came bringing food on donkeys, camels, mules and oxen. There were plentiful supplies of flour, fig cakes, raisin cakes, wine, olive oil, cattle and sheep, for **there was joy** in Israel* (1 Chronicles 12:40).

Jeremiah also prophesies such joy concerning a period of restoration:

> *They will come and **shout for joy** on the heights of Zion; they will rejoice in the bounty of the Lord—the grain, the new wine and the olive oil, the young of the flocks and herds. They will be like a well-watered garden, and they will sorrow no more* (Jeremiah 31:12).

There were certainly seasons and times of great joy, but this statement in Hebrews 1:9 was not just a time but an anointing. Indeed, this statement concerning Jesus was not just spoken of in Hebrews but was actually prophesied.

> *You love righteousness and hate wickedness; therefore God, your God, has set you above your companions by anointing you with the oil of joy* (Psalm 45:7).

The promise there adds one or two things that are valuable to look at. First, it states that this anointing sets you above your companions. That's what any anointing does, but the oil of joy sets you above because you are not relying on circumstance or times or seasons. It is given as an anointing!

Second, it states who gives it, *"God, your God."* The key to Jesus receiving it was truly relational, as is the key to any anointing. It comes from God, our God. But third and not least, He gains it due to His walk. *"You love righteousness and hate iniquity."* That's what the "therefore" is there for! Gained due to His walk. Gained due to His relationship. What an anointing!

Like all the anointings of Jesus, this is available to the believer. It is made real clear in Isaiah:

"to bestow on them...the oil of joy instead of mourning..." (Isaiah 61:3).

You can only bestow what you have! Jesus received the anointing and then bestowed it upon others who received His ministry and life. This clearly is to be a crown on our heads and a garment that is worn. It is nothing less than an anointing from the anointed One Himself.

Many of us have had moments of joy, seasons of joy, and impartations of joy, but to walk in its anointing? I can remember several specific times of such impartation. The first came as a young youth pastor when I was criticized publicly by a deacon. I was shocked and dismayed, but suddenly the oil of joy fell on me and ministered to me.

Several years later, I was in a half-night of prayer when it fell on the whole prayer meeting for hours. Who but God could have thought there would be a season like that in 1994, when it hit church after church and was carried for months. Yet, my greatest moment came when the Holy Spirit sat on me for hours and freshly baptized me. At that time, it came with an impartation of such joy. All were wonderful touches of His anointing. To have it bestowed and become part of our life and ministry exposes the potential that comes from our walk with Jesus. It clearly seems from Isaiah 61:3, that this is our potential. He gained it. He bestows it. It is ours in faith to receive it.

Circumstance cannot dictate this anointing. Nehemiah was trying to communicate that to the weeping inhabitants of Jerusalem. That was just a moment of feasting. What of a lifetime of being under His anointing?

9

ANOINTED WITH
FRESH OIL

I f we carefully study the life and ministry of David, we will discover he had more than a unique anointing. He saw the Lord and called Him *"my Lord."*

> *The Lord says to my lord: "Sit at my right hand until I make your enemies a footstool for your feet"* (Psalm 110:1).

Now guess who he was talking about? David also saw New Testament worship in the Old Testament! Called, of course, the tabernacle of David and mentioned by James:

After this I will return and rebuild David's fallen tent. Its ruins I will rebuild, and I will restore it (Acts 15:16).

David experienced the joy of salvation, *"Restore to me the joy of your salvation and grant me a willing spirit, to sustain me"* (Ps. 51:12).

David actually called it the "Joy of your salvation." He seemed to walk a New Testament grace while living in the Old Testament and Old Covenant times. Look at this statement in the Psalm and quoted by Peter in Acts 2:28:

*You make known to me the path of life; you will fill me with **joy in your presence**, with eternal pleasures at your right hand"* (Psalm 16:11).

David says, *"You have shown me the path of life,"* and he follows that with, *"You give me joy in your presence."* Then, for the most amazing statement of them all, I like the King James Version of Psalm 16:11, *"at thy right hand there are pleasures for evermore."* David saw the right hand of God. He even spoke of the waves of the Spirit breaking over him.

Deep calls to deep in the roar of your waterfalls; all your waves and breakers have swept over me (Psalm 42:7).

This is a fascinating Psalm, written either by David for the sons of Korah—Levites who ministered in the tabernacle of David on the worship team—to minister or written by one of them. If written by one of the sons, they were on his team and under the same mantle. Wow! What a walk and what an anointing! David is the one who reveals the anointing of fresh oil.

You have exalted my horn like that of a wild ox;
fine oils have been poured on me (Psalm 92:10).

This is so important; that as David walked into a New Testament revelation and grace, he speaks of the anointing being fresh or constantly new. This is recorded more than one time in the New Testament. The Book of Acts speaks of constant infillings:

All of them were filled with the Holy Spirit and began to speak in other tongues as the Spirit enabled them (Acts 2:4).

Then Peter, filled with the Holy Spirit, said to them: "Rulers and elders of the people!" (Acts 4:8).

After they prayed, the place where they were meeting was shaken. And they were all filled

*with the Holy Spirit and spoke the word of God
boldly* (Acts 4:31).

We are also told in Ephesians, that we are to be constantly filled with the Spirit. "Do not get drunk on wine, which leads to debauchery. Instead, be filled with the Spirit" (Eph. 5:18).

The Greek word used for filled here is the word plēroō, which means to replete and cram full. One scholar said this means to be being filled. This word speaks of constantly being filled and crammed full. This takes a constant imbibing of the fresh life of God.

The word "fresh" to anyone who speaks the English language means not preserved but new. It also means not previously used. Fresh as used in the Hebrew in Psalm 92:10 means to be green and verdant, new and prosperous. The New International Version (NIV) calls the oil "fine oils," meaning the best and not the leftovers! David uses the same Hebrew word in verse 14 of the same Psalm, and it speaks of how it will "stay fresh and green" in the NIV; but the King James Version translates it "fat and flourishing."

Anointed with fresh oil quite simply means a constant replenishing of the anointing, not with yesterday's oil, but today's. As the title of a song states, "A New Anointing for a New Day." To stay green means the life of it is constantly keeping things fresh! To flourish means it brings forth constant fruit and to be fat! That means we are to overflow in it...to be in excess. "Verdant" means to be lush, new, like that of a new forest.

When changing the oil in your vehicle, have you ever noticed how it has lost its freshness and viscosity, and how the new oil has a totally different consistency? Why would the Church live on a yesterday's anointing when, as in everything God does, there is access to the new? The old-time Pentecostals had it right when they sang, "Fill me anew, fill me anew, Spirit of the Lord, fall afresh on me." And in another song, "Spirit of the living God, fall afresh on me." They knew too well that we cannot rely on the old but need to constantly be being filled.

When I first got saved and touched by God, I used to love the testimonies of so many when they spoke of being filled with the Spirit—until I realized some of them were testimonies of many years before! No fresh infillings. No new touches. I cried to the Lord, "Let me know the constant touch of Your hand, oh God!" I have enjoyed so many infillings of the Spirit and so many fresh touches and anointings. The results have always been the same—new vision, new life, new joy, and new power, etc. This is our inheritance. It belongs to the sons and daughters of God.

Those He plants, He plants not only in the house of God but alongside the river of God as was described in Ezekiel 47. That very passage uses the word "fresh" three different times in the NIV, as it speaks of being touched by the river. The only place it says that the water is not fresh is in verse 11, where the marshes were. No fresh water there, living on the residue of water from old rain and former touches when the river ran its banks!

> *But the swamps and marshes will not become fresh; they will be left for salt* (Ezekiel 47:11).

Let's not be a stagnant marsh that is filled with the old water—let's be where the river is flowing and have a fresh touch and fresh anointing! Actually, the Hebrew word that the NIV translates *fresh* is a word that means *healing and mending and causing to live.* Even salty water is made fresh. There is nothing stagnant where the waters of the Spirit flow!

It is impossible to speak of this anointing without speaking of the context of Psalm 92:10. Fresh oil renews strength, vigor, and passion. It exalts or causes us to rise up again and mount up again. It gets the stirrings back up and the sense of taking a new place or promotion. The next verse speaks of the rout of his enemies.

> *My eyes have seen the defeat of my adversaries;*
> *my ears have heard the rout of my wicked foes*
> (Psalm 92:11).

Such power and invigorating life. What a great promise!

I have always loved the Song of Solomon. I personally feel it is the story of the relational walk between Christ and the Church and is filled with truth and inspiration. In chapter 5 is an incredible revelation:

> *I slept but my heart was awake. Listen! My beloved is knocking: "Open to me, my sister, my darling, my dove, my flawless one. My head is drenched with dew, my hair with the dampness of the night"* (Song of Solomon 5:2).

The beloved of our souls is bringing the fresh dew of God, but it cannot be delivered if we will not open up. That is so like our Bridegroom. He has not just obtained and released the anointing but constantly brings it afresh and releases it afresh. Let's open the door of our life for

His fresh oil and fresh anointings, both in the church and as individuals. The anointing of fresh oil is another anointing that belongs to all. It is not a fivefold minister's anointing only, but a believer's anointing as well. Remember, He is the God of *"new every morning."*

> *Because of the Lord's great love we are not consumed, for his compassions never fail. They are new every morning; great is your faithfulness* (Lamentations 3:22-23).

Older ones of us will remember the day of the milkman coming daily bringing a new delivery of milk. Or even the mail carrier bringing the mail to our house daily. All we had to do is open the door and collect. Our God has provided freshness for us constantly from His throne of grace! We can avail ourselves by opening our door and receiving this freshness. "He *has* anointed me with fresh oil" and "He *will* anoint me with fresh oil."

10

ANOINTED TO PROSPER

Wow, is that a title to a chapter! Anointed to prosper. You mean to say that there is such an anointing? Indeed there is, and it is found in a very famous Psalm that both Christian and non-Christian can often quote by heart—Psalm 23, *"The Lord is my shepherd."* I mean, really? Does it not say in verse 1 that *"The Lord is my shepherd, I shall not want"*? Yes, it does! In fact, the Hebrew word here for "want" means *lack* or *abatement* or *decrease and fail*. Well surely lack is not just spiritual but material too? The real Shepherd cares for all our needs. Just follow the life of Abraham. We are told several things in Galatians:

Understand, then, that those who have faith are children of Abraham. Scripture foresaw that God would justify the Gentiles by faith, and announced the gospel in advance to Abraham: "All nations will be blessed through you." So those who rely on faith are blessed along with Abraham, the man of faith (Galatians 3:7-9).

First, we are told that when we believe we become Abraham's children in faith, also we are blessed alongside him through our faith. In other words, as his children we can become blessed as he was blessed. This would take another book to explain, but we cannot follow the life of Abraham without seeing that his blessing included prosperity! The story of Abraham shows this exceptionally well.

Now Lot, who was moving about with Abram, also had flocks and herds and tents. But the land could not support them while they stayed together, for their possessions were so great that they were not able to stay together (Genesis 13:5-6).

Not only was Abraham blessed, but Lot, who traveled with him, came under the same blessing. They both became so blessed that the land could not support the two of them together. They were so blessed and so prosperous that they outgrew the ability to stay in one place together. That is prosperity indeed!

The key to this blessing? Faith! We find out that not only is it our Shepherd's desire to bless us but, to find in the same Psalm, there is an anointing given for prosperity—surely this will quicken our faith to reach in for such blessing and prosperity!

Have you ever wondered why the church frequently cites Psalm 23 at funeral services? Of course, it is because verse 4 is so commonly known from the King James Version:

> *Yea, though I walk through the valley of the shadow of death, I will fear no evil: for thou art with me; Thy rod and thy staff they comfort me* (Psalm 23:4 KJV).

The mention of the valley of the shadow of death does it, but the *shadow* is not the reality! And again, who walks through death? Dead people don't walk, they are carried! It's the next verse that should awaken us.

> *You prepare a table before me in the presence of my enemies...* (Psalm 23:5).

Oh no! My enemies are watching me in Heaven? Really? Oh gosh, that sounds ominous, but the next statement is an eye opener.

...You anoint my head with oil; my cup over-flows (Psalm 23:5).

I need anointing in Heaven? What for? No! I believe it is for earth, especially this anointing. This word for "anointing" is the Hebrew word *dâshên,* which means *to be fat, to make fat, and to satisfy.* It is translated *to prosper* in two places in Proverbs:

A generous person will prosper; whoever refreshes others will be refreshed (Proverbs 11:25).

The greedy stir up conflict, but those who trust in the Lord will prosper (Proverbs 28:25).

Another verse in Proverbs uses the same word translated to speak of full satisfaction:

A sluggard's appetite is never filled, but the desires of the diligent are fully satisfied (Proverbs 13:4).

This is the anointing to became fat and satisfied and to prosper. Now tie this anointing to the next statement in Psalm 23: *"...my cup overflows..."* (Ps. 23:5). An anointing that causes overflow. A blessing that satisfies and blesses others.

All anointing should be an overflow! It overflows into life and ministry. That is why we are *"anointed to...."* But anointed to overflow in prosperity, is an anointing to be able to bless others with our overflow of the goodness of God. That is such an anointing that so many have missed.

I presently live in San Antonio, Texas. Saint Anthony (San Antonio in Spanish) was the saint who gave himself to a vow of poverty. When we first arrived here years ago, many people in many places would say, "Ah, this is a poor city. Dallas and Houston and Austin are wealthy, but not this city." We stood and prayed and said, "Lord, the Christians are here! No more poverty!" This city is now one of the fastest growing in the nation with industry coming in from everywhere. The anointing to prosper has overflowed into our city!

I met a Muslim restaurant owner in Nottingham, United Kingdom. He said to me, "You are a Christian, yes? A minister?" He had found out as he observed us. Then he asked if we would do a mission to where he came from in Pakistan.

"Why?" I asked.

"Because, wherever the Christians go, there is prosperity!" A Muslim man had observed the overflow of the

Christian anointing and wanted his people to prosper. Now that is a testimony!

By the way, not only did Abraham and Lot prosper, but so did Abraham's son Isaac, to the point that a king asked him to move away.

> *The man became rich, and his wealth continued to grow until he became very wealthy. He had so many flocks and herds and servants that the Philistines envied him. So all the wells that his father's servants had dug in the time of his father Abraham, the Philistines stopped up, filling them with earth. Then Abimelek said to Isaac, "Move away from us; you have become too powerful for us"* (Genesis 26:13-16).

Our Shepherd wants us to prosper. He wants to anoint us with this oil and prosperity! How do we obtain it? Walk with the Shepherd, allowing His righteousness and name to be our portion as in Psalm 23.

> *He guides me along the right paths for his name's sake* (Psalm 23:3).

Trust in the Lord, even in *"the valley of the shadow of death"* circumstances—but then in faith reach in for such an anointing! It is our promise, too.

11

ANOINTED TO SEE

In every letter to the churches in the Book of Revelation, chapters 2 and 3, the statement is made, *"Whoever has ears, let them hear what the Spirit says to the churches."* There are seven churches, and the statement is made seven times. But one of the churches is told it needs more than to hear it also needs to be able to see.

> *You say, "I am rich; I have acquired wealth and do not need a thing." But you do not realize that you are wretched, pitiful, poor, blind and naked. I counsel you to buy from me gold refined in the fire, so you can become rich; and white clothes to wear, so you can cover your shameful nakedness;*

and salve to put on your eyes, so you can see
(Revelation 3:17-18).

The infamous Laodicean church, the church that felt it had everything, Jesus clearly told them they needed the ability to see because they were misguided about their true selves and where they were. The passage says that they thought they had it all together, "Rich and acquired wealth don't need a thing," but Jesus said they were in fact, blind and unable to see.

The ability to see is spoken of throughout the Scriptures. It is first mentioned in Genesis: *"Then the eyes of both of them were opened, and they realized they were naked…"* (Gen. 3:7). In this case, the opening of the eyes caused them to see their real state.

Elisha prayed that his servant would have an eye-opening experience:

> *And Elisha prayed, "Open his eyes, Lord, so that he may see." Then the Lord opened the servant's eyes, and he looked and saw the hills full of horses and chariots of fire all around Elisha* (2 Kings 6:17).

As a result, the servant saw what the Lord was doing versus what the enemy was doing.

Isaiah the prophet clearly knew that the people needed a revelation to see! Here are several examples, one of them quite shocking.

> *Hear, you deaf; look, you blind, and see! Who is blind but my servant, and deaf like the messenger I send? Who is blind like the one in covenant with me, blind like the servant of the Lord?* (Isaiah 42:18-19).

That is a wakeup call for today's Church. So many blindly going along doing what they do and missing all the Lord is doing.

In this second example, the Lord gives a prophetic command:

> *See, the former things have taken place, and new things I declare; before they spring into being I announce them to you* (Isaiah 42:9).

And then, the third example:

> *See, I am doing a new thing! Now it springs up; do you not perceive it?* (Isaiah 43:19)

You need to be able to see what God is no longer doing and see what He is doing!

Paul says in Romans that we need to understand the times. How can we understand without the ability to see?

> *And do this, understanding the present time:*
> *The hour has already come for you to wake*
> *up from your slumber, because our salvation*
> *is nearer now than when we first believed*
> (Romans 13:11).

The Laodicean church is so like the church of today, caught up in themselves. They felt being wealthy was being blessed by God. Sound familiar? The result? A lukewarm and spiritually blind church. The answer? The eyesalve of Revelation 3:18. The King James Version adds a wonderful word, "anoint," to its translation: "*...and anoint thine eyes with eyesalve, that thou mayest see*" (Rev. 3:18 KJV).

In the original Greek, this word "anoint" once more means *to rub with oil and besmear* the eyes. So there is anointing from the Lord Himself to see. He clearly lets them know that they need to come to Him for it and to buy it. Buy it? How do we do that? First, it means that the anointing is costly, which it is. It cost the Lord everything; and even though given freely, it costs us to give up of ourselves to gain it and walk with it.

Second, we need to apply the anointing to see. Without it we stay as we are. But what an anointing! To see as He wants us to see! See what? See ourselves correctly, see the church correctly, see what the Spirit is saying and doing. See what He is saying and doing in the churches. See prophetically. An anointing of seeing! What realms of vision and ministry.

Elisha's servant actually saw the heavenly hosts, when he saw what was revealed in Second Kings 6. Elisha had words of knowledge. Isaiah and David saw into Heaven. It is limitless what we might experience as the anointing to see is released fully into our lives. For just a few examples: Elisha had multiple words of knowledge, even seeing his servant talking to Naaman in Second Kings 5:26. Isaiah had visions of Heaven in Isaiah chapter 6; David in Psalm 110 and Psalm 16. There are numerous biblical illustrations, personal illustrations, and also historical illustrations of men and woman of God who see.

Personally, I have had dreams and visions and revelations. For example, I have had visions of God's outbreaks before they came and visions of sicknesses to be healed that brought faith to the hearer. I have been blessed with visions of babies to be born—but in fact they had not yet been conceived—and when spoken out, the person later conceived. What an anointing that sees into the heavenly realm, sees God's purpose, and brings faith when declared! Even as a young man just born again, before I was aware of my call into the ministry or even aware there was an anointing, I was given a vision of myself ministering under the anointing. I was touched by the anointing to see. Then later, the anointing was imparted to me and, as a prophet, I have been blessed to see and see and see.

Yet this anointing is not just offered to prophets, but to the leader of the church of Laodicea and indeed the whole church. The letters were to the churches—the believers within the church. The anointing is to the church itself, the whole church of Jesus. Of course, it will work and operate differently according to giftings, but it is part of our God-given right that we can gain the anointing to see as the Lord wants us to see.

12

ANOINTED TO BE HEALED

The anointing to be healed is a deep and awesome truth. The Old Testament reveals purposes for anointing, particularly in regard to anything dedicated to God. The priests were anointed to be dedicated to God.

> *After you put these clothes on your brother Aaron and his sons, anoint and ordain them. Consecrate them so they may serve me as priests* (Exodus 28:41).

> *Anoint Aaron and his sons and consecrate them so they may serve me as priests* (Exodus 30:30).

And then in Exodus 40:9-15, anointing both the tabernacle and its operations are covered as well as the priests. All to be consecrated to God for use, and the anointing made it not only acceptable but usable. So then quite simply, from the basis of this truth, the purpose of all anointing is to consecrate to God and then to devote the person, the ministry, the tabernacle, or its utensil to its purpose. We, the tabernacle of God, along with our gifts, etc., anointed in consecration—anointed in function.

When we understand this great revelation of being anointed to God and for God, we discover an anointing in the New Testament that seems to be different from other New Testament anointings—the anointing to be healed! James tells us that there is an anointing in the church unto healing.

> *Is anyone among you sick? Let them call the elders of the church to pray over them and* ***anoint them with oil*** *in the name of the Lord* (James 5:14).

The ingredients of this are imperative, look at the statement, *"Anoint them with oil in the name of the Lord."* Quite simply, dedicate those who are sick to the Anointed One for the purpose of being healed.

For this anointing to be released, we must look at the God-given format in this following statement:

And the prayer offered in faith will make the sick person well; the Lord will raise them up. If they have sinned, they will be forgiven. Therefore confess your sins to each other and pray for each other so that you may be healed. The prayer of a righteous person is powerful and effective (James 5:15-16).

The King James Version adds the word "fervent," to this last statement: *"The effectual fervent prayer of a righteous...."* Let's look at some of the ingredients of this format in James 5:14-16:

- Faith calls for the elders.

- Faith of the elders prays, trusting in God's healing power but also knowing they have the authority and anointing to do so.

- The confession and healing of sin must be released first. Please notice here the *"to each other"* that is involved.

- We all have this authority and anointing as believers.

- The anointing unto healing with oil is paramount and key. We devote to God and dedicate for the purpose of healing.

The fervency of prayer is then involved, with the context revealing the prayers of Elijah.

> *Elijah was a human being, even as we are. He prayed earnestly that it would not rain, and it did not rain on the land for three and a half years. Again he prayed, and the heavens gave rain, and the earth produced its crops* (James 5:17-18).

So, this operation is totally different from the laying on of hands or the use of gifts of healing. They are both releasing anointing in faith and gift. This, however, is anointing a person in devotion to God for the purpose of healing, then praying to the Lord fervently and in faith that this dedication is an acceptable sacrifice and will more than catch His attention. It is His divine format being fulfilled! The elders, devoted and consecrated to the Lord to lead, then from their anointed office can administer the prayer with the anointing oil. The fervency comes from our understanding of who He is, what He has said, and our desire for such a person to be healed.

Who does this healing belong to? It belongs to anyone sick among us. It belongs to the whole church! If the whole church would catch this truth, how many would be healed today?

13

THE HAND-OF-
GOD ANOINTING

There are statements, particularly in the Old Testament, where we are told, "The hand of God" or "the hand of the Lord" came upon people, often momentarily or for a season or task. Perhaps this verse in the King James translation is the most famous of these: *"And the **hand of the Lord** was on Elijah; and he girded up his loins, and ran before Ahab to the entrance of Jezreel"* (1 Kings 18:46 KJV).

The NIV version says, "The **power of the Lord** came on Elijah...." Both are actually correct.

Jesus Himself speaks of the ministry of just the finger of God: "But if I drive out demons by the **finger of God**, then the kingdom of God has come upon you" (Luke 11:20).

The disciples, in the Book of Acts, asked God to stretch out His hand to heal: "Stretch out your hand to heal and perform signs and wonders through the name of your holy servant Jesus" (Acts 4:30).

In other words, manifest Your power! The hand of God and the finger of God are all different dimensions of the manifestations of His power and glory.

The hand of God coming upon an individual manifests a moment when God, in His power, touches or uses the person. It is none other than a momentary anointing. In Elijah's case, it enabled him to run supernaturally, as revealed in First Kings 18:46. In Elisha's case, to prophesy creatively:

> Elisha said..."But now bring me a harpist." While the harpist was playing, **the hand of the Lord** came on Elisha (2 Kings 3:14-15).

In the Book of Ezra, the hand of God is mentioned several times and gave Ezra protection and favor. It came at different times and had different manifestations. The disciples in Acts 4 were praying for such a manifestation in a greater dimension, yet the Book of Acts tells us the apostles did great miracles; so we can conclude they were also talking about it coming upon them. Let's look at this passage in First Corinthians 12:7: *"Now to each one the manifestation of the Spirit is given for the common good."*

There we find the Greek word *phanerōsis*, which means *an exhibition or manifestation.* It seems the Holy Spirit is exhibiting not just a set anointing but sometimes a momentary anointing. The first time I heard of this was when I was a child. My father had told me he was called upon to give a speech in a religious setting and had felt this strange power come upon him. He knew that the Holy Spirit had fallen on him for a moment. It was many years later when he was baptized in the Holy Spirit, as mentioned in an earlier chapter.

This hand of God was also evidenced in Acts where we are told that Paul was enabled to do extraordinary miracles. The King James version uses a great word "wrought," which means *worked.* This was a powerful manifestation of God, for a season of time. *"And God wrought special miracles by the hands of Paul"* (Acts 19:11 KJV).

The reason I added this chapter is so important. The whole purpose for this book is to broaden our horizons... take off our limits on what anointings are available. This hand-of-God anointing itself is multidimensional. Why? Because the Holy Spirit can use any vessel in any manner He so chooses.

> *All these are the work of one and the same Spirit, and he distributes them to each one, just as he determines* (1 Corinthians 12:11).

The beginning of First Corinthians 12, speaking of the Holy Spirit, says this:

> *There are different kinds of gifts, but the same Spirit distributes them. There are different kinds of service, but the same Lord. There are different kinds of working, but in all of them and in everyone it is the same God at work* (1 Corinthians 12:4-6).

Those last two verses, the King James version expresses so well:

> *And there are differences of administrations, but the same Lord. And there are diversities of operations, but it is the same God which worketh all in all* (1 Corinthians 12:5-6 KJV).

"Differences of administrations" and "diversities of operations." All worked by the Spirit. There are no limitations to what He can do if there is a willing servant around! We might be anointed into an office, we might be anointed to do certain things, we might even operate in certain giftings through His anointing—but never rule out the hand of God coming upon us at any time and in any season. I have seen those who don't prophesy suddenly touched and, BANG, a creative word of God is released. Those not used particularly in healing I have seen suddenly quickened by God to heal. Sometimes these are demonstrations for a moment, a place, or a particular situation—He moves in His own way.

I even had it suddenly happen to me when confronted by a demon while visiting in Dallas as a young man. I had a powerful, momentary touch of God with supernatural faith and a lady was delivered in an instant. The old-time Pentecostals used to call these touches of God, *unctions*. Sometimes they are for a moment or season, sometimes the individual reaches in and the unction becomes a resident anointing. There's no end to the possibilities of the Holy Spirit's anointings and manifestations.

14

GAINING ANOINTING

I t is amazing indeed—as the Holy Spirit reveals more and more of what is available to us as believers and as sons and daughters of God. So much. Such a great treasury. No wonder Psalm 23 says, *"You prepare a table before me in the presence of my enemies"* (Ps. 23:5).

The Song of Solomon speaking of the Bridegroom leading His bride, *"Let him lead me to the banquet hall, and let his banner over me be love"* (Song of Sol. 2:4).

But how do we gain all that God has for us in this matter of anointing?

First, let us not forget or ever rule out the sovereignty of our God. He calls and endues, but we are for sure involved in the greatness of dimension and fullness of flow.

Thirst and desire are mentioned throughout the Bible, ranging from David, who walked in such anointing, and even First Corinthians where we are told to desire the gifts, *"Follow the way of love and eagerly desire gifts of the Spirit, especially prophecy"* (1 Cor. 14:1).

The Greek word used for "desire" in this statement has within it *a longing, a lusting and a zealousness in wanting to gain*. In fact, it also means *to be jealous over*. The anointing is for those who are not willing to do without it, are prepared to pray for it, and zealously go after it. But the anointings come from the Anointer! To want what He does without wanting Him is missing the point completely. Jesus makes clear the thirst should be for the life of God Himself.

> *On the last and greatest day of the festival, Jesus stood and said in a loud voice, "Let anyone who is thirsty come to me and drink. Whoever believes in me, as Scripture has said, rivers of living water will flow from within them"* (John 7:37-38).

The overflow comes from that! The best gift is the Holy Spirit Himself. We are called into fellowship with Him.

> *Therefore if you have any encouragement from being united with Christ, if any comfort from his love, if any common sharing in the Spirit, if any tenderness and compassion* (Philippians 2:1).

> *May the grace of the Lord Jesus Christ, and the love of God, and the fellowship of the Holy Spirit be with you all* (2 Corinthians 13:14).

The following are some ways to gain anointing:

1.   You can gain sovereign anointing as in Acts 2 and other places, where He is clearly manifesting His outpouring. In this way, many people have walked into revival outpourings and caught the anointings that were being manifested. What happened in Toronto, Canada, in 1994 is a clear example. What happened in Pensacola, Florida, another. I have heard testimony after testimony of many people and entire churches that were affected and anointed through these outpourings. In fact, our church moved into a seven-day-a-week outpouring because I went into the presence of such an outpouring many years ago.

Basically, the river is at flood stage and those touched by it can gain it and walk it in their lives.

2.   You can gain anointings wherever and whenever the ministry of the Spirit is in operation. The whole chapter 3 of Second Corinthians and the beginning of chapter 4 focus on this subject. We are told it is more glorious in operation than when the glory of God appeared to and through Moses.

> *Now if the ministry that brought death, which was engraved in letters on stone, came with glory, so that the Israelites could not look steadily at the face of Moses because of its glory, transitory though it was, will not the ministry of the Spirit be even more glorious? If the ministry that brought condemnation was glorious, how much more glorious is the ministry that brings righteousness! For what was glorious has no glory now in comparison with the surpassing glory. And if what was transitory came with glory, how much greater is the glory of that which lasts!* (2 Corinthians 3:7-11)

This ministry transforms us from glory to glory.

And we all, who with unveiled faces contemplate the Lord's glory, are being transformed into his image with ever-increasing glory, which comes from the Lord, who is the Spirit (2 Corinthians 3:18).

A glory, it says, which can be manifested by us! When the Holy Spirit is moving where He is in manifestation, there is the potential of impartation of anointings: *"Now the Lord is the Spirit, and where the Spirit of the Lord is, there is freedom"* (2 Cor. 3:17).

Or as the King James Version says, *"Now the Lord is that Spirit: and where the Spirit of the Lord is, there is liberty"* (2 Cor. 3:17 KJV). Liberty, I love that word! It is the same Greek word used in Romans speaking of the liberty of the children of God.

That the creation itself will be liberated from its bondage to decay and brought into the freedom and glory of the children of God (Romans 8:21).

Ministry to the sons and daughters of God could be a great way of saying this. Paul makes it very clear that he carried this ministry, *"Therefore, since through God's mercy we have this ministry, we do not lose heart"* (2 Cor. 4:1).

This is not just sovereign, people are used by the Spirit and impartation can come as He uses them and they manifest His ministry.

3.   You can be anointed by the prophetic. This fact is found in both Old and New Testaments. Samuel anointed David:

> *So Samuel took the horn of oil and **anointed** him in the presence of his brothers, and from that day on the Spirit of the Lord came powerfully upon David. Samuel then went to Ramah* (1 Samuel 16:13).

Samuel also anointed Saul:

> *"Then Samuel took a flask of olive oil and poured it on Saul's head and kissed him, saying, 'Has not the Lord **anointed** you ruler over his inheritance'"* (1 Samuel 10:1).

Elijah anointed Elisha:

> *"So Elijah went from there and found Elisha son of Shaphat. He was plowing with twelve yoke of oxen, and he himself was driving the twelfth pair. Elijah went up to him and threw his cloak around him"* (1 Kings 19:19).

Paul shares in the anointing and gifts that came to Timothy through the prophetic, *"Do not neglect your gift, which was given you through prophecy when the body of elders laid their hands on you"* (1 Tim. 4:14).

We should always be open to the release of impartation that comes through the prophetic. There is such a power in the prophetic. As the Lord reveals to Ezekiel, "Then he said to me, 'Prophesy to these bones and say to them, "Dry bones, hear the word of the Lord!"'" (Ezek. 37:4).

The result? The prophetic word released the power and authority of the Lord. The bones did what the prophet said. Why? Because the Word of the Lord has such creativity. Prophets both by office and the carrying of what God says cause a release of His hand and anointing. The second part of Ezekiel's prophecy was that the wind, or breath, of God would come.

> *Then he said to me, "Prophesy to the breath; prophesy, son of man, and say to it, 'This is what the Sovereign Lord says: Come, breath, from the four winds and breathe into these slain, that they may live'"* (Ezekiel 37:9).

When we prophesy according to the Word of the Lord, the wind of God moves. The man known as "Mr.

Pentecost," David Du Plessis, was imparted to by Smith Wigglesworth while in South Africa. Smith Wigglesworth is perhaps one of the most famous known Pentecostal ministers of the last century. He is known for multiple miracles. In fact, in a church I personally pastored in Bristol, one of the main leaders was born as a result of Smith ministering to her barren mother. I have other friends that saw many of his miracles. His book, *Ever Increasing Faith,* is a classic.

David Du Plessis became famous during the great outpouring of the Holy Spirit among many churches worldwide that were non-Pentecostal.

4.   You can be anointed by other anointed people. Examples start in the Old Testament with Moses laying hands on Joshua in Deuteronomy and continues throughout the New Testament.

> *Now Joshua son of Nun was filled with the spirit of wisdom because Moses had laid his hands on him. So the Israelites listened to him and did what the Lord had commanded Moses* (Deuteronomy 34:9).

Anointed people impart from their anointing, such as the apostles:

Then Peter and John placed their hands on them, and they received the Holy Spirit. When Simon saw that the Spirit was given at the laying on of the apostles' hands, he offered them money (Acts 8:17-18).

...and then Paul: *"When Paul placed his hands on them, the Holy Spirit came on them, and they spoke in tongues and prophesied"* (Acts 19:6).

All were imparting from their own anointing. Elijah, although anointing as a prophet, actually releases also from his own anointing.

When I was a young minister, I was ordained by the Assembly of God in the United Kingdom. It was a huge ordination service. As the leaders of the movement came out to pray, there was a man there who carried a specific mantle, and I asked the Lord, "Let him pray for me!" Sure enough, he moved down the line and imparted to me alone. I received not just ordination but also his anointing.

So many testify that they received their present anointing when a man or woman of similar anointing prayed for them. For many others, as they served a particular person, the mantle of their anointing cast more than a temporary shadow and they caught the same anointing. In fact, one of my best friends, who is used in healing, studied under one of the anointed healers of today. Another friend, in response to a dream, not only sat under this man but invited him into his church and the anointing was passed on.

5. You can be anointed if you minister to the anointed one. A tremendous promise is given in First Samuel:

> *I will raise up for myself a faithful priest, who will do according to what is in my heart and mind. I will firmly establish his priestly house, and they will **minister before my anointed one** always* (1 Samuel 2:35).

There was one coming who would minister before His Anointed One always. We realize that person was David as we proceed to study the Scripture. David's life before God and his worship brought him before that Anointed One always. The result? An anointed one, who was quite unprecedented in his time. You cannot minister before the Anointed One without the anointing of His presence coming on you. Nothing replaces time in His presence. As one of my spiritual mentors once said, "Time in His presence brings His presence into your times."

6. You can be anointed through fellowship with the Holy Spirit. Did you notice that the disciples had touched Jesus' anointing even before Jesus poured out the fullness into their lives? The reason? They walked in fellowship with the Anointed One. If we spend time with the Holy Spirit, it won't be long before who He is will start to touch our lives! Benny Hinn testifies that when he saw and heard Kathryn Kuhlman, he cried out for such a fellowship himself. The results I think are evident.

I myself have had three different visitations while crying out to know the Holy Spirit. Also, as the word "fellowship" means, offer yourself to copartner with the precious Spirit in His mission that He wants to use you in.

7. You can be anointed by being around anointed people. We know of Elisha and we see Timothy and Joshua. These three walked with the anointed. Throughout the ages it has always been the same. Either walk with or spend time with anointed people. Be around when they minister. It stirs up a thirst and a faith concerning their anointings.

These are a few suggestions regarding gaining anointing. I believe intensely that God often stirs you to what He wants you anointed in. Pray for it, thirst for it, and get around it. Don't let go. The Lord is more willing to impart than we are to push Him to gain.

There is a word in the English language that is not too often used. The word is "receivability." It came to us during a season of outpouring. It means quite simply, *is it receivable?* Often used to check the quality of a claim, etc., in our case, do we have a receivable spirit? Are we open to receive? Are we ready to receive? I placed this here because so many ask for the anointings, but they are not in a place or of an attitude to receive what they ask, nor are they expectant that it will come.

Truly Hebrews says, *"So, as the Holy Spirit says: 'Today, if you hear his voice'"* (Heb. 3:7). That means God is the God of today. We must keep that in mind when seeking the anointing. Always be ready for Him to speak and touch your life.

15

WALKING IN CONSTANT ANOINTING

Even though Romans 11:29 in the King James Bible clearly states that the gifts and callings of God are *"without repentance,"* the NIV version translates the phrase as *"irrevocable."* Wonderful indeed, but the anointing must be tended to! In the tabernacle, the priest had to tend to lamps and keep them burning continually.

> *The Lord said to Moses, "Command the Israelites to bring you clear oil of pressed olives for the light so that the lamps may be kept burning continually"* (Leviticus 24:1-2).

To keep the anointing fresh, we must tend to it. Minister to it and learn to walk in it. Kathryn Kuhlman was heard on more than one occasion referencing how to treat the ministry of the Spirit.

First, we must honor the anointing, *"But you have an anointing from the Holy One, and all of you know the truth"* (1 John 2:20). We must honor who this anointing comes from—the Holy One! We must treat it as holy and given for holy use, not to be used for self or gain. Also, we must walk a walk of holiness—given to God, given to His purpose, and walking as His vessels. This will truly affect the anointings on our lives.

To tend to something clearly means to minister to it. The priests had to make sure there was plenty of oil, which of course means they should be being filled with the Spirit *continually* as is the meaning in the instructions given: *"Do not get drunk on wine, which leads to debauchery. Instead, be filled with the Spirit"* (Eph. 5:18).

The priests also had to make sure the lamps were kept clean and the wicks were trimmed, removing the old and keeping the ministry pure.

In the Book of Acts, there is so much on ministering to the anointing; but perhaps no better statement than found in Acts 13:2: *"While they were worshiping the Lord and fasting, the Holy Spirit said...."* Many Bible versions translate this portion of the verse this way: *"As they were ministering unto the Lord and fasting."* They were ministering to Him whether in worship or prayer or fasting. They were ministering to the Anointed One, which keeps the anointing real and fresh and holy.

The results were clear. After they worshiped, or ministered, *"The Holy Spirit said,"* which confirms worship and ministry brings the release of the life of the Spirit. There is a promise given in First Samuel 2:35:

> *I will raise up for myself a faithful priest, who will do according to what is in my heart and mind. I will firmly establish his priestly house, and they will minister before my anointed one always.*

That verse states that *"they will minister before my anointed one always."* To minister before Him and minister to Him enables us to walk in His anointings.

Several times in the New Testament the word "fellowship" is mentioned regarding the Holy Spirit:

> *Therefore if there is any consolation in Christ,*
> *if any comfort of love, if any **fellowship** of the*
> *Spirit, if any affection and mercy* (Philippians
> 2:1 NKJV).

> *May the grace of the Lord Jesus Christ, and the*
> *love of God, and the **fellowship** of the Holy*
> *Spirit be with you all. Amen* (2 Corinthians
> 13:14).

The word "fellowship" comes from the Greek word, *koinonia*. It means *to partner with* and *be in communion with* and *share in common with*. Simply put, we need to walk with and partner with the Holy Spirit on a daily basis. After all, He releases the anointings. I believe the deeper the fellowship, the greater release of the anointings. In his book *Good Morning Holy Spirit*, Bennie Hinn references this deep, sweet fellowship that he developed. I think perhaps the anointing has been quite evident in his life and ministry.

To stay grateful and never take anything for granted is surely part of our Christian life; but to become overfamiliar with the anointing and always expect it to be there for our use, is a dangerous area to walk in. The Bible clearly states that the Holy Spirit can be quenched:

"Do not quench the Spirit" (1 Thessalonians 5:19).

The context of this admonition speaks of taking light of His manifestations and ministry. That verse warns people of their response! How much more the attitude and demeanor of the vessel. The parable in Matthew 25 about the five wise and five foolish virgins covers this attitude of taking His anointing for granted so well. No oil. When there is no oil for an anointed vessel, this is no light matter!

The title of this chapter is Walking in Constant Anointing. The anointing is His to give, but ours to walk in. The letter to the Colossians in the New American Standard Bible translation speaks so clearly, *"Therefore as you have received Christ Jesus the Lord, so walk in Him"* (Col. 2:6).

In other words, whatever you receive from the Anointed One, walk it, live it, and make it a lifestyle. It's your walk to walk.

Let's walk!

SUMMARY

Paul clearly tells us what is needed to know God and His purposes better: *"I keep asking that the God of our Lord Jesus Christ, the glorious Father, may give you the Spirit of wisdom and revelation, so that you may know him better"* (Eph. 1:17).

A Spirit of wisdom and revelation and hearts that are opened—I believe that revelation on any subject within the Word is given by the Author Himself. The truths are there, but they need to be clearly seen. My prayer is that this book will open your eyes to some of the limitless potentials that are offered in the realm of anointing.

The whole subject came as a result of the Holy Spirit speaking to me. Initially I shared the original thoughts that came, but when I looked deeper and prayed more, of course more came. As mentioned in the beginning of the book, I feel like Oliver Twist, in Charles Dickens' book, crying out, "Please sir, can I have some more?" But rather than dealing with an austere master, we deal with One who longs for His children to participate in all that He has. Indeed, *"Christ in you, the hope of Glory!"*

Abraham was told in Genesis that whatever he saw was his:

> *The Lord said to Abram after Lot had parted from him, "Look around from where you are, to the north and south, to the east and west. All the land that you see I will give to you and your offspring forever"* (Genesis 13:14-15).

If we see it, we can reach out and gain it. But we must first see it. I like the prophetic statements made by Isaiah:

> *See, the former things have taken place, and new things I declare; before they spring into being I announce them to you* (Isaiah 42:9).

> *Forget the former things; do not dwell on the past. See, I am doing a new thing! Now it springs*

*up; do you not perceive it? I am making a way
in the wilderness and streams in the wasteland*
(Isaiah 43:18-19).

See! May we see more, yet more and yet more. May the church of today walk in its fullness as purposed by our benevolent and gracious Father.

Think on this:

*Blessed are those whose strength is in you,
whose hearts are set on pilgrimage. As they pass
through the Valley of Baka, they make it a place
of springs; the autumn rains also cover it with
pools* (Psalm 84:5-6).

Blessed are they who have set their hearts to go after all that God has for them. Verse 6 speaks of springs or wells that come as a result of their journey.

The promise of Jesus in John 7 is so clear:

*On the last and greatest day of the festival, Jesus
stood and said in a loud voice, "Let anyone
who is thirsty come to me and drink. Whoever
believes in me, as Scripture has said, rivers of
living water will flow from within them"* (John
7:37-38).

Diversity of revelation and manifestation. His anointings being released—and released and released!

Out of his fullness we have all received grace in place of grace already given (John 1:16).

From the very fullness of His grace, may we receive the fullness of His blessings and grace!

ABOUT THE AUTHOR

Dennis Goldsworthy-Davis is a strong prophet who ministers both prophetically and apostolically throughout different parts of the world. Known to many as a governmental prophet, he is a strong declarer of the present word of God and imparts the presence of God wherever he goes. He truly carries the Spirit of Revival with him. Being a strong believer in transgenerational impartation, he has fathered many sons in the Kingdom.

Converted in 1973 from a life of violence and drugs, Dennis was fathered in the Lord by an apostolic minister who traveled extensively throughout the world.

Dennis first ministered as a youth pastor and then later pastored in several areas of the United Kingdom. In 1986, he relocated to San Antonio, Texas, and became part of a vibrant apostolic team. In 1990, Dennis pioneered Great Grace International Christian Center (GGICC).

He currently travels and ministers under the umbrella of Open Wells Ministries and serves as senior minister of GGICC in San Antonio. He is connected to various other apostolic ministries in the United States and Europe.

He and his wife, Christine, have two daughters, Sasha and Hannah, and three grandchildren.

Experience a personal revival!

Spirit-empowered content from today's top Christian authors delivered directly to your inbox.

Join today!
lovetoreadclub.com

Inspiring Articles
Powerful Video Teaching
Resources for Revival

Get all of this and so much more, e-mailed to you twice weekly!

LOVE TO READ CLUB
by **D DESTINY IMAGE**